S OMETHING IS very wrong with our political culture today. That's one of the few areas of agreement in this era of contentious and uncivil debate.

We need to restore a climate in which we can productively debate across the political divide and decide upon different policies, leaders, and paths forward. We want to create an environment where more good people seek to get involved in leading our communities and country.

This Broadside explores one overlooked phenomenon that helps fuel the lack of civility in the debate between sides, makes it harder to distinguish facts from falsehoods, and discourages good people from getting involved.

This phenomenon is the privilege afforded to the progressive worldview by many of the most influential institutions of our society.

You may feel like you are already well

familiar with the "progressive privilege" concept, which sounds a lot like liberal media bias, and has been explored in many books and forums. It isn't a great revelation to hear that journalists at major newspapers and television channels are disproportionately Democrats. But the extent of those leanings may be surprising: One study by the Center for Public Integrity looking at donations to presidential campaigns by working journalists in 2015 and 2016 finds that 96 percent went to Hillary Clinton. Indiana University professors find that for every journalist who self-identifies as a Republican, there are four who identify as a Democrat. While media bias plays a role in this phenomenon, progressive privilege is different.

Similarly, the overwhelming dominance of liberal professors on college campuses, where there are ten professors registered as Democrats for every one Republican professor, and the softer echo of this split in our public K–12 schools, contributes to progressive privilege.

> *Progressive privilege is helping to drive our country into two camps, where there is no expectation of fair treatment and respectful debating of the facts between the sides.*

But the bias in these institutions is just one aspect of a larger problem.

Progressive privilege is a phenomenon that pervades art, music, fashion, and entertainment advertising, as well as our news and political culture. It is a similar phenomenon to those commonly referred to as white privilege and male privilege, and one that we increasingly recognize also applies to other factors such as sexuality, religion, and class. Privilege isn't just about being a member of a majority but encompasses subtle forms of discrimination that set expectations for what is normal, what is good, what is just, and what is not.

As a conservative, I have a particular interest in raising awareness and diminishing the power of progressive privilege since it creates burdens for me and those who share my philosophy.

Yet conservatives are not the only group that would be better off if progressive privilege were to lose its influence. Liberals and moderates would benefit as well.

Progressive privilege is helping to drive our country into two camps, where there is no expectation of fair treatment and respectful debating of the facts between the sides. It weakens Democrats and progressive activists by discouraging the vetting of their leadership and policy ideas. It also weakens Republicans and conservative activists by encouraging them to reject criticism – even just criticism – of their leaders and ideas as simply being the result of blind bias.

We want good people to feel free to speak

their minds, offer their ideas, and get involved in public life with the expectation that they will be evaluated fairly, even if rigorously, and not denigrated based on stereotypes, associations, and falsehoods.

To make this a reality, we need to recognize how stereotypes and prejudices of all forms impact our actions and behaviors and marginalize some by defining them as outside of what is "normal." Becoming woke to the power of privilege is the first step in freeing ourselves from it and creating a healthier political environment and a fairer, stronger country.

PART ONE
WHAT IS PRIVILEGE?

The civil rights, women's rights, and gay rights movements succeeded in ending legal discrimination based on race, gender, and sexual orientation. Just as important, they made discrimination socially unacceptable. Today, in the United States, there are few charges more dreaded or damaging than being called bigoted.

Yet even though outright discrimination has been rendered illegal and has become less prevalent, we've still failed to achieve Dr. Martin Luther King Jr.'s vision of a society where people are judged solely by the content of their character rather than on the color of their skin – or their sexuality, gender, religion, or other status. Equality may be protected under the law, but it seems far off in practice.

Some scholars have begun to explore how factors and institutions other than legal and explicit social discrimination make it more difficult for some to flourish. Specifically, scholars have come to recognize the favoring of certain groups over others in terms of societal expectations for what is normal, the existence of lingering stereotypes that frame how people and their actions are perceived, and other traditions that provide some with unearned benefits and others with unearned burdens.

This is what's come to be commonly referred to as "forms of privilege."

Knapsacks of Privilege

In 1988, women's studies professor Peggy McIntosh wrote a working paper entitled, "White Privilege and Male Privilege: A Personal Account of Coming to See Correspondences through Work in Women's Studies." The paper was published by Wellesley College's Centers for Women and launched the contemporary discussion of privilege.

McIntosh begins by describing her frustration as a women's studies professor with "men's unwillingness to grant that they are over privileged." This leads her to consider privileges that she enjoys as a white person and how they impact her life experience and outcomes:

I have come to see white privilege as an invisible package of unearned assets that I can count on cashing in each day, but about which I was "meant" to remain oblivious. White privilege is like an invisible weightless knapsack of special provisions, assurances, tools, maps, guides, code-books, passports, visas, clothes, compass, emergency gear, and blank checks.

As a part of her awakening to this privilege, she lists "forty-six ordinary and daily ways in which I experience having white privilege, by contrast with my African American colleagues in the same building."

This list includes:

➤ I can, if I wish, arrange to be in the company of people of my own race most of the time.

➤ I can turn on the television or open to the front page of the paper and see people of my race widely and positively represented.

➤ When I am told about our national heritage or about "civilization," I am shown that people of my color made it what it is.

➤ I can be sure that my children will be

[8]

given curricular materials that testify to the existence of their race.

> Whether I use checks, credit cards, or cash, I can count on my skin color not to work against the appearance that I am financially reliable.

> I can talk with my mouth full and not have people put this down to my color.

> I am never asked to speak for all the people of my racial group.

> I can expect figurative language and imagery in all of the arts to testify to experiences of my race.

> I can choose blemish cover or bandages in "flesh" color and have them more or less match my skin.

Today, more than thirty years after McIntosh developed this list, some items no longer belong or are much less prevalent than they were in the 1980s.

In 1988, 80 percent of the US population

were white. Today, it is about 61 percent and white people's share of the population will continue to decline. We now commonly see people from a variety of racial backgrounds, as well as religions and sexualities, positively depicted on entertainment programming and the news. Curricula at schools have been made more inclusive of racial perspectives other than those of white Europeans, as well as of subject matter involving various ethnicities, religions, and lifestyles. It has become much

Scholars have recognized the favoring of certain groups over others in terms of societal expectations for what is normal and the lingering stereotypes that frame how people and their actions are perceived.

more commonplace to see people from a variety of backgrounds in leadership roles at workplaces, governments, and universities.

But certainly, much of the white privilege that McIntosh observed continues today. Some argue persuasively that what McIntosh referred to as white privilege was as much a result of her income and class as her skin color. McIntosh is highly educated, wealthy, and well connected both by birth and marriage.

Writing in *Quillette*, author William Ray eviscerates McIntosh's failure to recognize the limits that being white has in serving as a source of privilege:

Very few of the people reading this article – whatever the color of their skin – will have even the vaguest idea of the comfort and privilege in which Peggy McIntosh grew up and to which she has since become accustomed.... But even though the lifetime of privilege McIntosh has experienced is almost certainly due to her wealth and not the colour of her skin, she nevertheless found a way to share this irksome burden with the illiterate children of Kentucky coal miners, the hopeless peasants of the Appalachians, poor single mothers struggling to make ends meet on welfare, and the vast majority of whites in the United States and throughout the world who never had the chance to attend Radcliffe or Harvard. She simply reclassified her manifest economic advantage as racial privilege and then dumped this newly discovered original sin onto every person who happens to share her skin color. Without, of course, actually redistributing any of the wealth that, by her own account, she had done nothing to deserve.

Today, people debate and discuss different gradations of privilege and where different sources of privilege flow from. There is privilege associated with age, with older people being considered out of touch and the young being dismissed as too limited. While the privilege associated with heterosexuality is widely recognized, privileges associated with being a part of a couple or having children receive less attention but are also real.

Not only is being able bodied and minded (or lacking a handicap) associated with an increased level of privilege but so is having an attractive physical appearance. People who are overweight, have bad skin, have missing or discolored teeth, or are too short in the case of men or too tall as women all face disadvantages, while those with more traditional physical beauty enjoy advantages. Yet, in some cases, being too physically attractive can actually become its own burden, especially for a woman whose intellect or other attributes can be overshadowed by her beauty.

Academics trying to raise awareness of privilege created a matrix to help students recognize how privilege works, the types of privilege that people might unknowingly enjoy, and even hierarchies of privilege. Buzz-Feed and other online sources invite people to take quizzes with a series of questions about their life experiences to calculate how much privilege they enjoy.

As our culture has become increasingly "woke," or aware of how majority cultures oppress other cultures and enjoy unearned rewards, being a member of these majorities can itself be seen as a disadvantage and membership in a victim class can actually carry its own benefits and privileges.

Regardless of one's opinion on the merits of Senator Elizabeth Warren's claims to have Native American heritage, it is clear that she thought there was an advantage to being something other than simply a Caucasian woman. Speaker John Boehner emphasized having grown up in a larger family and working in his father's bar to demonstrate his difference with other more privileged white males. Similarly, Vice President Joe Biden consistently sought to make his middle-class background sound as modest as possible. Perhaps this is as simple as understanding that since Americans tend to root for underdogs, many want to be seen as some kind of underdog themselves.

Assigning privilege can be taken too far, though, and become a form of stereotyping. Whiteness and heterosexuality may generally confer privileges in American society, but that doesn't mean that every white heterosexual enjoys much meaningful privilege or hasn't faced his or her own challenges and hardships. Encouraging people to fixate on their status as a member of a disadvantaged

As our culture has become increasingly aware of how majority cultures oppress other cultures, membership in a victim class can actually be seen as carrying its own benefits and privileges.

group or compete over the level of disadvantage of their social group can be counterproductive both for social cohesion and for individual advancement. Our goal should be to see and value people as individuals rather than to focus on their identity as a member of various identity groups.

However, this doesn't render the entire concept of privilege useless or wrongheaded. Greater awareness of how society creates expectations for what is considered "normal," and how it treats those who fail to conform with those expectations, can help encourage people to be more inclusive and kind.

The process of identifying these privileges confers benefits not just on those who lack them but also on those within the privileged class. Discounting other cultures or people with different backgrounds or beliefs creates a less-informed, -interesting, and -innovative world for everyone involved. It also prevents people from reaching their full potential and maximizing their contributions to our society, leaving everyone worse off.

This is why it is so important to acknowledge how one form of privilege – the privilege enjoyed by those with a progressive political worldview – is being overlooked when we consider the different forms of privilege. Progressive privilege not only leads to the unfair treatment and stereotyping of those who do not share the progressive worldview but also impacts debates of politics and policy, marginalizing potential solutions and encouraging greater polarization and social strife. Progressive privilege deserves consideration.

PART TWO
HOW PROGRESSIVE PRIVILEGE WORKS

Peggy McIntosh described her journey of becoming aware of how her whiteness (which we now recognize as being better understood as also a product of class, income, and education status) conferred a variety of unrecognized and unearned benefits: "My schooling gave me no training in seeing myself as an oppressor, as an unfairly advantaged person, or as a participant in a damaged culture." To build an understanding of the privilege she had failed to recognize and appreciate, she developed her list of the privilege she experienced during her daily life.

I myself recognize that I enjoy tremendous privileges as a result of my background, demographic characteristics, and lifestyle: certainly, I am considered very privileged on any privilege matrix or hierarchy.

As I became aware of how political orientation confers its own privileges and shares similarities with other privilege classifications, I began my own list inspired by McIntosh's to note how progressive privilege manifests in my everyday life:

> When I open a women's magazine, I expect to see female leaders of progressive causes represented as positive and aspirational figures. I do not expect to see female leaders of my own political party or persuasion represented at all, and if they are represented, I expect to see them belittled.

> When I turn on the television for entertainment, I expect to see the people who

share my political philosophy depicted as bigoted, hypocritical, and out of touch.

➤ I expect to see ads for consumer products that showcase their affinity for progressive political causes.

➤ When I participate in an apolitical social event, I expect people to make fun of members of my political party.

➤ When I attend a social event, I recognize that it would be inappropriate or considered socially awkward to bring up my political beliefs.

➤ When someone I don't know who works outside the field of politics asks what I do and I reveal that I am conservative, I have to be prepared that they might assume I am a bigot.

➤ I expect my children to be taught by teachers who do not share my political beliefs and who not only teach with a progressive slant but also encourage my children to think that conservative ideas

are wrong and motivated by an indifference or malice toward vulnerable people
and the environment.

> If my children go to college, they will be
taught almost exclusively by progressive
professors who are often overtly hostile
to conservative beliefs.

> I can count on mainstream reporters
asking me if they can describe the women's
organization I represent as a "conservative
organization," while, in the same story,
I know they won't similarly qualify progressive or liberal women's organizations
by their ideology. Those will just be
"women's organizations."

> When I or someone from my organization
speaks on a college campus about how
public policy impacts women, I know the
women's center at the college will not
promote the event.

> When mainstream media outlets cover
policy debates, they usually will frame

the conservative side as being motivated by prejudice or indifference to the poor and the progressive side as championing fairness and seeking to help the poor. They will rarely consider conservatives' claims, and supporting data, suggesting that their policies would better help the poor.

› I can expect my conservative colleagues who are not white to be marginalized by their racial group and the media, with the implication that they are betraying their race and shouldn't be considered part of it.

› I can expect that fact checkers will scrutinize conservatives' claims and ideas more rigorously than they will the claims and ideas of members of different ideologies.

› If a conservative makes a joke or statement that could be construed as offensive or prejudiced, most media will assume that he or she is bigoted rather than just awkward.

> I take it as a given that supposedly neutral newspapers of record, major wire services, and network television will consistently present information that favors progressives and minimize the stories of wrong-doing by their own leaders.

> When someone who claims to be a Republican commits a crime or does something offensive, they will immediately be identified by their political leanings. If I do not disavow their statement, people will assume that I support them.

> I can depend on the content I hear on government-funded public television and radio to overwhelmingly feature progressive views.

> When I watch a Hollywood award show or interview with a celebrity, I can expect to be given a lecture on the virtues of progressive political ideas and hear a denigration of conservatives' viewpoints.

> When I turn on a daytime or morning

talk show on a major network, I can expect to hear progressive messages and see progressive leaders lauded.

> ➤ I expect the media to inflate the number of people who attend progressive events and rallies, while ignoring or under-counting attendance at conservative events.

> ➤ When the media talks about women voters, I can expect that who they are really talking about are the women voting for Democrats. And when they do decide to analyze a group of non-Democratic women, they will offer such explanations as the women being manipulated by men in their lives or driven by prejudice.

As I was developing this list, I recognized that some aspects of the privilege I encounter may in part be a result of geography. Most of my education and work life has occurred in the Northeast, urban areas, and even Europe. People in rural and deep red states may have very different experiences in their social

When I open a women's magazine, I do not expect to see female conservative leaders represented at all, and if they are represented, I expect to see them belittled.

interactions. In fact, in those areas it could be that conservatives enjoy the privilege of being seen as "normal" when discussing politics in social settings. Similarly, those working in certain industries or around certain religious communities may find that more-conservative politics and expectations are the norm.

And one can certainly find other examples where progressives are demeaned or stereotyped in our culture or media outlets are slanted to favor Republican viewpoints, but when these things happen, the media sources tend to be publicly recognized as "conservative" outlets. The mainstream entertainment, fashion, media, and education culture that dominates the United States offers a progressive worldview but is rarely labeled as such, promoting progressive privilege broadly and shaping our national conversations and what is considered publicly acceptable everywhere.

Progressive privilege impacts everyone but places particular unearned burdens on conservative leaders – particularly women. Consider the different treatment that female Democratic candidates and political officials can expect to receive in comparison with their female Republican counterparts.

A female Democratic politician can expect:

> major women's media to give her awards, invite her to events, and feature airbrushed photo spreads that make her look more stylish and attractive than she may actually be;

> daytime talk shows to interview her in formats that humanize her and show her as relatable, rather than challenging her on policy questions or her experience;

> the media to cite her as evidence of women's growing power and progress toward true equality;

> mainstream reporters to present her policy positions in at least a neutral, and more likely favorable, light and if she makes an error or does something inadvertently offensive, they will allow that the error was an aberration from her usual conduct;

> and to be described as a rising star within her party when appointed to a position of power.

On the other hand, a female Republican politician can expect:

> major women's magazines to ignore her;

> to be challenged on her policy agenda and background when interviewed on daytime talk shows or by mainstream reporters, with little discussion of her personal life or background – and when

there is such a discussion, it will feature an emphasis on the ways in which she is privileged or conforms with conservative stereotypes;

➤ any errors she makes or things she does that might be inadvertently offensive to be taken as emblematic of larger biases or deficiencies associated with conservatives;

➤ not to be seen as evidence of women's rising power but rather as a threat to it;

➤ when elevated to a position of prominence in her party, to be dismissed by the media as window dressing being used by Republican men to appeal to women;

➤ and to be viciously caricatured by *Saturday Night Live* and comedians, to have her personal appearance denigrated, and to be hounded out of restaurants and other public places in cases where she is very successful.

Specific examples of progressive privilege in

media, the news, and its many manifestations can be found at iwf.org/progressiveprivilege.

The next part will show how progressive privilege impacts everyone and makes society worse.

PART THREE
PROGRESSIVE PRIVILEGE –
WHY IT MATTERS

Like anyone who faces unfair negative stereotyping, conservatives who are made to feel outside of the norm and denigrated by the mainstream culture are likely experience a host of emotions including defensiveness, insecurity, and reduced self-worth.

Survey research provides a window into how conservatives differ from progressives in their perception of how their views are received, and the impact their perception has on their willingness to engage in political discussions.

Research commissioned by the Independent Women's Forum in January 2019 looking at a national representative sample shows that those who self-identify as "very conservative" are twice as likely as those who identify as "very liberal" to strongly agree that they have to "keep their views to themselves" or "hide my views." They are also twice as likely to report having "lost friendships" due to politics.

Yet progressive privilege doesn't just impact those denied this knapsack of unearned benefits. It has far-reaching consequences for all members of our society.

Those who self-identify as "very conservative" are twice as likely as those who identify as "very liberal" to strongly agree that they have to "keep their views to themselves."

Increased Polarization and Distrust

Many conservatives, frustrated by progressive privilege and the liberal media bias that seems to consistently distort events to favor progressive ideas, now wholly reject the mainstream media and listen exclusively to their own explicitly conservative media sources.

Conservatives don't want to be preached to by the *New York Times*, hear a preening network anchor spin a stellar jobs report into something lackluster, or listen to what the lopsided panel on *The View* have to say about the latest, soon-to-be-retracted revelation in the Trump-Russia probe. We instead follow the news trending on our own social media feeds or on our favorite websites, which we know sees the world and issues the way that we do.

The bifurcation of the media is an understandable development and the availability of a wide variety of news and information sources that offer different perspectives is a tremendous improvement from the days when only a few powerful individuals at New York City–based media companies got to dictate what news was on television and who got to tell the stories of the day. Many of the more conservative news sources are ones that I highly value, and that seek to fairly analyze events and information that they see as underreported or unfairly characterized by the mainstream press.

But conservative news sources, like progressive ones, have their own biases that influence their coverage and analysis. News sources with a political slant are less likely to highlight data or events that do not support their own policy prescriptions and more inclined to seek benign explanations for the misdeeds of their leaders and organizations.

In his important recent book *Them: Why We Hate Each Other – and How to Heal*, Nebraska senator Ben Sasse details this phenomenon and the natural human tendency to seek what's called confirmation bias – prioritizing content and information that confirms "we are right" about what we believe and think we know. Just as the media is influenced by their own political biases in deciding who to condemn and who to give the benefit of the doubt and which stories are important, readers and viewers increasingly can also indulge their biases, patronizing news sources that tell them what they want to hear.

This impacts how we evaluate policies and candidates. We are more likely to blindly support members of our team and believe the worst charges against our opponents. Because we are no longer in the habit of focusing on facts, we elevate those on our team who excel at demagoguing the other side rather than those with the best ideas, strongest records and backgrounds, and most persuasive arguments.

Sasse describes the growing tribalism in this country and the troubling tendency of people to embrace the idea that "the enemy of my enemy is my friend." We cheer on those people in our ranks who are most willing to stand up to – and even unfairly demonize – the other side even when they are deeply flawed and aren't fighting fairly or representing our best ideals and principles.

Otherwise nice people end up participating in social media mobs and slinging insults at the latest enemy on the other side. We fail to recognize the truth, as Senator Sasse so aptly puts it, that "sometimes the enemy of your enemy is just a jackass," and that those on the other side of most political arguments are actually our friends, neighbors, and countrymen – not our enemies.

Progressive privilege doesn't benefit progressives and harm conservatives so much as it pushes us further apart and makes any type of consensus or progress less likely. This is bad for the country and for individual communities but also bad for us as individuals, as it isn't healthy or helpful to be perpetually angry and to think badly about half of your countrymen.

It's easy to assume that progressive privilege at least politically benefits the Left. The progressive mainstream media glosses over scandals involving liberal politicians and cherry-picks data to support progressives' policy agenda, which can be a political advantage. But this bias can also backfire against them.

For example, the Women's March on Washington attracted more than a million women to its first event in Washington, DC. These women were upset by the election of President Donald Trump because of his personal statements about women and what they believed his presidency would mean for women and America. The Women's March leaders received numerous awards and fawning press coverage from mainstream outlets such as *Glamour*, *TIME* magazine, CNN, the *New York Times*, the *Washington Post*, and countless other media outlets. Concerns raised by conservatives about some of the leadership's positions and statements, such as those expressed by Linda Sarsour, were ignored or dismissed as illegitimate.

It wasn't until nearly two years after the women's movement launched and partici-

Because our political system has become less based on facts and a fair evaluation of policy preferences and more based on tribalism, many good people are opting out of politics entirely.

pants started raising concerns about their leaders' associations with extremist views and calling for their resignation that the press bothered to report on their problematic public statements and associations, leading public support for the Women's March to crumble. Had the press been more neutral and publicly reported some of these well-known problems earlier, the nonprofit organization likely would have taken more swift action and replaced the movement's leadership with people who better reflected the activists' concerns and beliefs.

Instead, the Women's March effectively alienated many of its most prominent partners and has been able to attract just a small fraction of participants for its 2019 events. This is an instance when progressive privilege has backfired on the progressive cause.

Discouraging Political Participation

Many news stories following the 2018 election celebrated the growth in the number of women elected to serve in the House and Senate, but noted that this overwhelmingly occurred on the Democrat side: While the number of female Democrats rose from eighty-one to one hundred and six from 2018 to 2019, the number of Republican women in federal elected office actually fell from twenty-nine to twenty-one.

Certainly, the Republican Party shares some of the blame for failing to support and elevate its very worthy female members and candidates. The Republican Party has also failed to make a strong and compelling case for its policies directly to women voters consistently and effectively, hurting their electoral prospects across the board.

However, progressive privilege also contributes to this phenomenon and discourages more conservative women from getting involved in politics. As described in the previous part, women running as Republicans can expect to receive different treatment than those running as Democrats. So, is it really such a surprise that fewer conservative women run for office?

This is particularly true for conservative women but applies to conservative men, too. Because our political system has become less based on facts and a fair evaluation of policy preferences and more based on tribalism, many good people who might make great policy makers but aren't interested in throwing mud or having mud thrown at them are opting out of politics entirely. Our last two presidents, President Trump and President Obama, have both likened politics to street fighting and boasted of their willingness to deploy bigger, more lethal weapons. Many good people aren't particularly interested in taking part in a street fight. Who could blame them?

If we want to find the best paths forward and elevate positive leaders to bring the country together, we need to reduce progressive privilege.

CHECKING PROGRESSIVE PRIVILEGE

Progressive privilege is a problem, and it harms everyone. The good news is that greater awareness of it is the first step to rolling back its influence. Here are ways that you can help check progressive privilege.

Learn to recognize bias in what you see, read, hear, and say.
It's important to become active consumers of the information, entertainment, and culture around us. Many of us have been taught by our schools and human resource departments to consider that even our words and

behaviors that might not be actively discriminatory or offensive might make people feel marginalized. Start becoming aware of how progressive privilege manifests around you and how it might make people who don't share the ideology feel.

Model the behavior you want to experience.
Stereotyping people based on political beliefs is wrong. If we want people to stop demonizing conservatives, we should also take care not to unfairly denigrate others.

We should reserve strong words and condemnation for those who truly embrace hateful philosophies, but recognize that these are a small minority of our country and our parties. We don't want the terrible behavior of a few extremists to be used to tar the entirety of those who share our political philosophy. Therefore, we should likewise avoid picking on the most extreme examples of bad behavior on the other side and trying to brand them as a whole.

Call out instances of progressive privilege.
Educate friends and family by pointing out examples of progressive privilege that you witness together. This doesn't require criticizing or attacking the source of the privilege. It can be as simple as pointing out how it's strange that no conservative women were included (again!) among *Glamour's* "Women of the Year," or noting the frequency with which Netflix shows feature white, Southern, Christian men, whom some viewers might associate with conservatism, in the roles of criminals, hypocrites, virulent racists, or misogynists.

Consider commenting on the media's mistreatment on its website or writing a letter to the editor when you see a particularly egregious example of progressive privilege. Many reporters and producers likely aren't aware of how they stereotype conservatives and the harm it causes. If they recognized that they were being unfair to this group, they'd likely stop.

Engage in respectful discussions with people of different beliefs and ideologies.

We need to break out of our echo chambers, not just in terms of what we click on online but in terms of whom we engage in political conversations. When having a political conversation with somebody of a different viewpoint, it's important to remember that reaching an agreement isn't the goal. Neither is scoring your own political points.

The goal should be to first gain information and an appreciation for why someone believes or feels as they do and only after that to share your own perspective. Avoid dredging up the worst examples of behavior or most extreme positions of figures admired by the person you're talking with. There are plenty of bad apples on both sides, but they don't represent any ideology or political party as a whole. They certainly don't represent the friend, colleague, neighbor, or acquaintance that you are engaging in conversation. Look for common ground in the goals you share with the other person and your joint desire to create a better future for the people you care about.

No society will ever be completely free of bias. America stands out for its dedication to working to create a society where everyone – regardless of their race, ethnicity, sex, gender, religion, sexuality, physical limitations, income, and educational status – is treated as an individual, not stereotyped as a member of group. We should be seeking to include "political ideology" on this list and to make

---

We can diminish how progressive privilege marginalizes some while conferring benefits on others by becoming aware of its prevalence around us and talking about it openly.

---

sure that an individual's political affiliation is not used to denigrate them.

We can diminish how progressive privilege marginalizes some while conferring benefits on others by becoming aware of its prevalence around us and talking about it openly. This would be an important step in creating a more truly diverse and inclusive society where civil and productive political discussions thrive.

First American edition published in 2019 by Encounter Books,
an activity of Encounter for Culture and Education, Inc.,
a nonprofit, tax exempt corporation.
Encounter Books website address: www.encounterbooks.com

Manufactured in the United States and printed on
acid-free paper. The paper used in this publication meets
the minimum requirements of ANSI / NISO Z39.48–1992
(R 1997) (*Permanence of Paper*).

FIRST AMERICAN EDITION

LIBRARY OF CONGRESS CATALOGING-IN-PUBLICATION DATA
IS AVAILABLE

10 9 8 7 6 5 4 3 2 1

SERIES DESIGN BY CARL W. SCARBROUGH